COOL CATS

Manx

by Christina Leaf

BELLWETHER MEDIA · MINNEAPOLIS, MN

Note to Librarians, Teachers, and Parents:

Blastoff! Readers are carefully developed by literacy experts and combine standards-based content with developmentally appropriate text.

Level 1 provides the most support through repetition of high-frequency words, light text, predictable sentence patterns, and strong visual support.

Level 2 offers early readers a bit more challenge through varied simple sentences, increased text load, and less repetition of high-frequency words.

Level 3 advances early-fluent readers toward fluency through increased text and concept load, less reliance on visuals, longer sentences, and more literary language.

Level 4 builds reading stamina by providing more text per page, increased use of punctuation, greater variation in sentence patterns, and increasingly challenging vocabulary.

Level 5 encourages children to move from "learning to read" to "reading to learn" by providing even more text, varied writing styles, and less familiar topics.

Whichever book is right for your reader, Blastoff! Readers are the perfect books to build confidence and encourage a love of reading that will last a lifetime!

This edition first published in 2016 by Bellwether Media, Inc.

No part of this publication may be reproduced in whole or in part without written permission of the publisher. For information regarding permission, write to Bellwether Media, Inc., Attention: Permissions Department, 5357 Penn Avenue South, Minneapolis, MN 55419.

Library of Congress Cataloging-in-Publication Data

Leaf, Christina, author.
  Manx / by Christina Leaf.
    pages cm. – (Blastoff! Readers. Cool Cats)
  Summary: "Relevant images match informative text in this introduction to Manx. Intended for students in kindergarten through third grade"– Provided by publisher.
  Audience: Ages 5-8.
  Audience: K to grade 3.
  Includes bibliographical references and index.
  ISBN 978-1-62617-312-5 (hardcover : alk. paper)
  1. Manx cat–Juvenile literature. 2. Cat breeds–Juvenile literature. I. Title.
  SF449.M36L43 2016
  636.8'22–dc23

                                        2015029921

Table of **Contents**

At first, Manx look like ordinary cats. However, many do not have tails!

The **breed** has long or short hair. Long-haired Manx are called Cymrics.

The breed's name comes from the Isle of Man. Short-haired Manx have hunted mice on the island for **centuries**.

Isle of Man

The rest of the breed's history is unclear. People believe their missing tails are a **mutation**.

Some say **Vikings** brought long-haired cats to the island. They think these cats **bred** with **native** cats to make Cymrics.

No matter how they came to be, Manx are lovable pets!

There are four different kinds of Manx. Rumpies are the most famous. They are tailless.

rumpy

riser

Manx with small bumps for tails are risers.

Stumpy Manx have short tails.

stumpy

longy

Those with full tails are longies.
They help make healthy kittens.

Manx **coats** are soft and thick.
The long-haired coats feel **silky**.

Manx Coats

solid

tabby

calico

bi-color

Both lengths come in many colors and patterns.

Manx have round heads with big cheeks. Their bodies are strong and **stocky**. Long back legs help Manx jump high. Some hop like rabbits!

Manx Profile

round head and cheeks

stocky body

short or
no tail

Weight: 8 to 12 pounds (4 to 5 kilograms)

Life Span: 12 to 18 years

Playful and Protective

Manx are playful. They speed around the house after toys.

Some play fetch!

19

These cats love people. They follow their owners like dogs.

Manx watch over their families.
They growl at signs of danger!

Glossary

bred—produced offspring

breed—a type of cat

centuries—hundreds of years

coats—the hair or fur covering some animals

mutation—a new form of something that has changed

native—originally from a specific place

silky—soft, smooth, and shiny

stocky—thick in build

Vikings—a group of people from Denmark, Norway, and Sweden that attacked the coasts of Europe between the years 800 and 1000

To Learn More

AT THE LIBRARY

Britton, Tamara L. *Manx Cats.* Edina, Minn.: ABDO, 2011.

Landau, Elaine. *Manx Are the Best!* Minneapolis, Minn.: Lerner Publications Co., 2011.

Perkins, Wendy. *Manx Cats.* Mankato, Minn.: Capstone Press, 2008.

ON THE WEB

Learning more about Manx is as easy as 1, 2, 3.

1. Go to www.factsurfer.com.

2. Enter "Manx" into the search box.

3. Click the "Surf" button and you will see a list of related web sites.

With factsurfer.com, finding more information is just a click away.

Index